CIA
Flaps and Seals
MANUAL

Edited By
John M. Harrison

CIA Flaps and Seals Manual
Edited by John M. Harrison

Copyright © 1975 by John M. Harrison

ISBN 10: 0-87364-039-X
ISBN 13: 978-0-87364-039-8
Printed in the United States of America

Published by Paladin Press, a division of
Paladin Enterprises, Inc.
Gunbarrel Tech Center
7077 Winchester Circle
Boulder, Colorado 80301 USA
+1.303.443.7250

Direct inquiries and/or orders to the above address.

Visit our Web site at www.paladin-press.com

Table of Content
Basic Flaps And Seals Techniques
Index

FOREWORD

With a reasonable investment in time and effort the average person can become a good all-round F&S (flaps and seals) operator in investigative work. This does not mean to say that the average person should undertake surreptitious entries of highly protected items of mail with the level of training outlined in the following. Only persons who specialize in that type of activity should attempt that. Nevertheless, the greater part of clandestine mail intercept work will involve surreptitious entires into mail that can readily be manipulated by the methods outlined in the following.

There are three basic factors that must be observed in this work. They are:

Carefulness
Cleanliness
Skill

The operator must consciously consider every move that his hands and fingers make and use every sense to observe the results of these moves. This is not hard to remember when beginning this work but can be overlooked after the operation has become routine or when there is pressure to hurry. Carelessness can have no place in this kind of work.

The phrase "Cleanliness is Next to Godliness" is very appropriate to F&S work. Handling of paper causes its appearance to change. Dust on the working surface, oily hands, or dirty tools and equipment will leave their traces on the material that has been manipulated. Cleaning the work area and washing the hands immediately prior to the work is mandatory. Cigarettes and beverages in the vicinity of the work area are prohibited. Consider this type of work as major surgery and yourself as the patient. Clean up accordingly before each job.

Inasmuch as this type of work involves precision movements and pressures and they must be executed manually and under time limitations, a high order of skill is required for success. The amount of pressure and the manner in which it is applied is quite critical in some cases. The amount of steam that can be tolerated by the subject material is of extreme importance in others. There is no known way to measure these factors and others with machines and to control them accordingly. Skill and

1

experience are used instead. These things are brought to a certain level in training courses but must be developed further and maintained by the individual.

The following material contains descriptions of how the various phases of the work are performed. They are not to be considered as a substitute for an expertly supervised training course. They are, however, an excellent aid for such a course and can subsequently act as refresher material when there is a time lapse between the training course and operational work.

The photographs were made against a dark background for clarity and contrast. This should not give the operator the impression that a clean blotter is not used in all cases as the working surface. The primary value of the photographs is to show the position of the material, the fingers, and the hands in the various operations. There is invariably more than one way to doing anything and that is true of this work. The processes presented herewith have been used successfully over an extended period of time in operational work. The operator should, however, always consider that there may be a better method and to attempt to develop them on non-operational material. He should always use the greatest of care and consideration before applying new techniques to operational work.

This material is to be considered highly sensitive and must be handled and stored accordingly.

ARRANGEMENT OF THE WORKING AREA

There are a variety of ways in which the operator may set up his work area. The one shown is good for general work in a restricted space. Where more space is available, all equipment may be spread out in a line on a longer table. The general rule of thumb is to set things up more or less in the order in which they will be used, to have the tools and materials most frequently used closest at hand, and to have materials (especially fluids) located so they cannot damage the operational material if spilled.

Good illumination and ventilation is important but the work area should be rather dark when a UV examination is made. Heavy curtains or drapes that can be put over the windows are suitable in most cases and are a good idea anyway for security reasons.

There should be power available for the steamer, electric iron, and the UV and IR lamps. The switch for regular room illumination should be accessible from the working area. Unless the power line is extremely stable, an automatic voltage regulator should be used on the line to the photo lights to avoid non-uniform exposures.

With regard to the photo copy table, there should be sufficient space on each side of the copy stand to allow photographed and unphotographed papers to rest. This is particularly important in this kind of work as papers must be replaced in their envelope in the same order in which they were removed.

Clean water should be used for all processes where it is required except for steaming. A small stoppered bottle of distilled water is recommended for the work area.

Liquids such as water, glue, and carbon tet should be poured into a work tray (Petrie dish) for use and should never be used directly from the bottle. In this way, impurities added to the liquids are not applied to other envelopes. The contents of the work tray are discarded after each session, tools should be cleaned and all swabs and other expendable items disposed of. It should be emphasized that the greatest of care should be taken to avoid contaminating one piece of work with material from another. Minute quantities of a different kind of glue, for example, might betray the surreptitious entry.

The work setup shown can be dismantled and dispersed readily. If an electric iron or fry pan is used instead of the "Hamburger Grill" the material by itself (except for tools and certain small special accessories) are not particularly sensitive and can be stored accordingly. In a domestic dwelling, a small concealment chamber can be devised for the sensitive items. This setup can be assembled with practice in less than five minutes and be ready for operation in whatever time it takes to get up steam, if such is required. The "Hamburger Grill" is very slow in coming up to temperature on 110 volts and an electric iron or similar device is therefore highly advantageous where setup time is limited.

It is well to provide a system for emergency destruction of all sensitive material in such a work setup. This might become necessary to avoid being apprehended in possession of incriminating evidence. The operational material and copies of it would be such evidence. Undeveloped film is easily destroyed by exposing it to a bright light. Letters and envelopes are best destroyed by burning. A container and an incendiary for such should be kept on hand. An efficient and clean burner should be used that has provision for collecting the ash.

A last item that can often be used to advantage is an interval timer with alarm. The timer can be used by the operator to remind him when the time is nearing to return the material to its normal channel. It is advisable to use an alarm that is not so loud that it will startle the operator so much that he will cause damage to his work.

A typical work setup for a domestic dwelling. The material shown is listed below approximately as it appears from left to right.

Leica IIIG
Cable Release
Circular Fluorescent Lamp
Lamp Power Supply (Now Shown)
BOOWU Leitz Copy Stand
 Electric Iron

Infra Red Lamp in Holder
Tongue Depressers 6 each
Petrie Dishes 2 X ½" 3 each
Camles Hair Brushes No. 1
    and No.2
Scissors

Opening Tools (wood and ivory) Albastone Powder (SS White)
Pincers Sketch Pad and Pencil
Carbon Tetrachloride 2 oz Steamer
101-X Glue Hamburger Grill
Photo-flo (Kodak) Ultraviolet Light
Cotton Swabs

Not shown is an automatic volate regulator (150 VA), a second UV light, a rubber mixing cup, a teaspoon measuring spoon and a spudging knife.

DESIGN OF OPENING TOOLS

The design of opening tools is not critical providing that the parts that come in contact with the subject material are smooth and are kept clean. There are certain points that it is well to keep in mind besides these. Ivory piano key blanks are good raw materials for tools for dry openings as they can be made smooth and of somewhat more intricate shapes than wood tools.

Ivory tools are not recommended highly for steam openings as they tend to condense water on their surfaces and to induce bleeding thereby. They may be used for steam openings, however, if special care is used to keep them dry.

Wood tools may be made from tongue depressers. The wood may be cleaned occasionally with fine sandpaper and will tend to absorb moisture during steam openings.

Both types of tools may be formed by sawing, filing and sanding. The shapes for two types are shown in the following drawings. The straight wood tool can be used for all types of work. The curved ivory tool is sometimes better for dry openings. The dimensions are primarily predicated by the average width of the glue line on envelope flaps.

Notice that the edges of the tools should not be sharp. This is to prevent cutting. The curved shoulders of the tool pushing the paper surfaces apart are the parts of the tool that do the work. The tip of the tool is made fairly sharp so that it may be used to lift the end of a strip of cellophane tape and in other similar types of applications where a sharp edge is required.

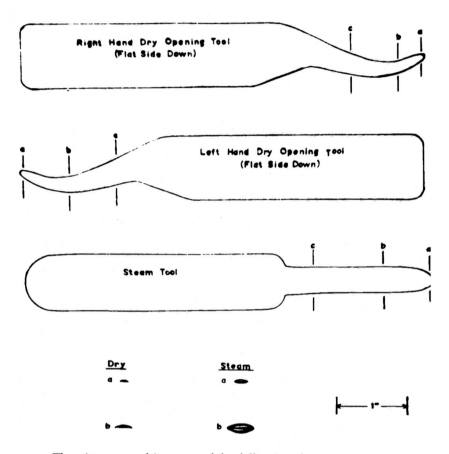

Right Hand Dry Opening Tool
(Flat Side Down)

Left Hand Dry Opening Tool
(Flat Side Down)

Steam Tool

Dry   Steam

a —   a ⬤

|— 1" —|

b —   b ⬤

The pincers used in some of the following descriptions are modified surgical hemostats. The facing jaw surfaces are smooth to avoid marking paper or metal. The exact dimensions are not critical. These pincers may be fashioned by grinding, filing, smoothing with emery cloth, and buffing. Certain types of tweezers might be used in place of these pincers with equal results.

The steamer shown is a commonly available vaporizer for medicinal use. It produces a jet of steam of a good intensity and size for this type of work. It has the disconcerting habit however, of allowing steam to escape from beneath the lid. The operator may be scalded by this and cause damage to his work. The operator may choose another steamer for his work as long as it does the job well. It is important to be sure that the steam leaves the jet nozzle at a sufficiently high temperature. Low temperature steam can cause too much setting of the material before it responds. Steam can be cooled by the type of material around the nozzle and the distance it travels to the nozzle. It is best to test a new steamer thoroughly on light weight as well as heavy envelopes before using it operationally.

DRY OPENINGS

Probably the most desirable way to open an envelope surreptitiously is by means of the dry method. There are, of course, many envelopes that will not respond to such a technique and these will probably have to be steamed or manipulated otherwise. Wherever possible however, the dry method should be used because when properly done it is nearly impossible to detect.

A successful dry opening is one where the glue separates into particles or layers, part of which remain on the flap and part on the body of the envelope.

It should be emphasized that the dry method should be abandoned with the first evidence that the envelope will not respond. Serious and obvious damage to the envelope can result if the operator persists in such cases.

Envelopes made of fairly hard paper into which the glue has had difficulty in penetrating will be the types most amenable to dry openings. Certain other envelopes are sold with very little glue on the flap and will also open easily without steam or water.

The dry opening technique is quite simple but can be the trickiest or most deceptive. The operator should use every sense to detect indications of damage when using this process.

A dry opening is performed by inserting the tool under the flap at the opening at the end of the envelope. The envelope is held lightly against the table top with the left hand and the opening tool is rocked in the manner illustrated with light pressure in the direction shown. When using the ivory tool a back and forth or sawing motion may be used to advantage. Remember to keep the pressure light and to listen and look for signs of damage. Occasionally the lower flap may open more readily than the upper so don't overlook the possibility of opening one side of the envelope instead of the entire top flap.

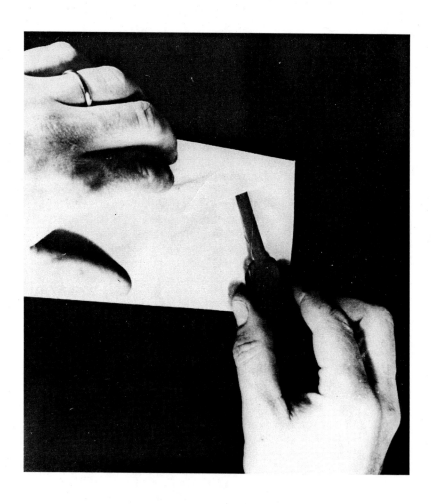

REMOVAL OF CELLOPHANE TAPE

Cellophane adhesive tape (Scotch Brand, etc.) may be removed from envelopes by the application of carbon tetrachloride. The procedures is described in detail in the following pages.

This type of tape will collect dust and dirt readily, so great care should be taken in handling it after it has been removed. In some cases new tape may be used to replace the existing tape if it is definitely of the same type as that removed. Rolls of various sizes should be kept on hand for this purpose. Great care should be taken to replace the tape in exactly the same position as it occupied originally and not to leave 'readable' fingerprints in the adhesive. It is possible to apply this type of adhesive without leaving fingerprints in it and it is also possible that some people might do this as a trap so make sure what the original tape looked like before replacing it.

Special attention should be paid to overlapping layers of cellophane tape. Cachets may be stamped partly on an envelope and partly on the back of the cellophane tape. The entire cachet can then be covered with another layer of cellophane tape. As the cachet will appear to be stamped wholly on the envelope it will be easy for the operator to inadvertently rub it off the back of the cellophane tape as he is removing the upper layer.

When replacing the cellophane tape in layers it is possible to leave a pocket of carbon tet layers. This cannot dry and will therefore leave evidence of an opening. Wet spots under the cellophane tape in the envelope should be allowed to dry before the tape is replaced.

NOTE: Carbon tetrachloride is highly toxic. It *must not* be allowed to get into cuts or scratches in the skin or to be in contact with extensive areas of the skin surface. It *must not* be inhaled in any quantity and if the user has any alcohol in his system this is particularly important. This chemical is very insidious and has killed many people. Once it is absorbed into the human system through the skin or the lungs there is no cure for it and the results are fatal.

To remove cellophane tape first pour a small amount of carbon tet into a Petrie dish. Hold the opening tool in the left hand as shown and apply carbon tet *to the envelope* near the tape with the brush in the right hand. Notice that the little finger of the right hand is holding the envelope about two inches off the table so that the carbon tet will flow under the tape. When the adhesive has softened the tape can be lifted up slightly from the paper tip of the tool.

As soon as enough tape has been lifted by the opening tool, grasp the tape with the pincers. Just hold a point of the tape to avoid leaving a mark in the adhesive. Apply more carbon tet allowing the weight of the envelope to pull it away from the tape. As brush marks can show up under flurescence be careful not to touch the tape with the brush. Let the carbon tet flow down the envelope to the adhesive.

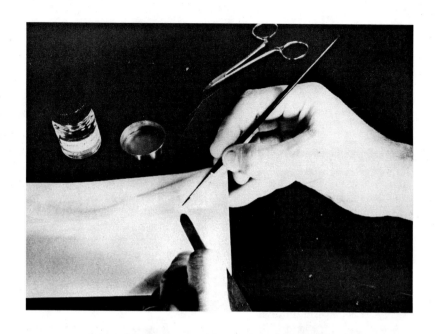

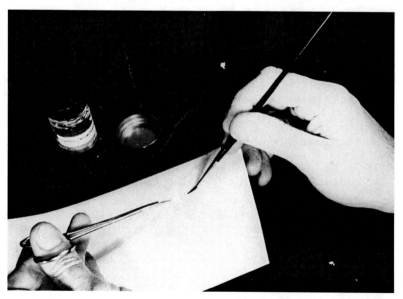

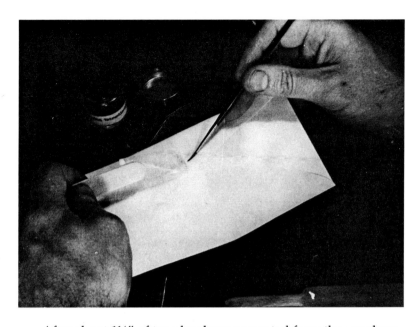

After about 1½″ of tape has been separated from the envelope it can be attached lightly to a tongue depresser. This should have a clean and smooth surface to avoid leaving marks in the adhesive. In this part of the process the tape is being pulled back by the left hand as the adhesive is softened. If the entire strip is removed a second tongue depresser may be attached to the other end of the strip of tape after it is removed from the envelope and the assembly of tongue depressers and tape can be set down on the table with the adhesive side of the tape up. It should be put far enough from the work area so that it will not accidentally be damaged. If one end of the envelope is to be opened, the tongue depresser shown in this picture may be held against the envelope with the left hand and the opening work performed with the right hand as usual. Avoid steaming the tape as it will change its appearance.

WET OPENINGS

Many types of glue used to seal envelopes are soluble or can be softened in water. Heat will sometimes facilitate or accelerate this process. Where the envelope will not respond in whole or in

11

part to dry opening attempts, water may be applied to the outside of the envelope over the glue line. Although steam is usually more effective than water, the water may be applied in small areas with greater control than can usually be exercised with steam. It should be mentioned that this type of opening is usually only made in conjunction with another, i.e., as an aid to a difficult spot in a dry opening attempt. The wet opening can also be used to advantage where carbon paper has been put inside the envelope as a trap, as steam will damage the carbon paper and water (under control) will not.

When using water, care should be taken to avoid wetting the ink on the envelope or the letter. The water should be applied carefully over the glue line. The envelope may be buckled in such a way that the letter will be held away from the back of the envelope. When part of the flap has been opened, a folded blotter may be inserted into the envelope between the back of the envelope and the letter to protect the letter from being wet. If there is ink (writing or a stamp) on the back of the flap at the glue line the wet opening may be impossible at that spot. The ink may be tested with a damp cotton swab. If there is any indication of feathering of the ink the wet opening cannot be used there.

In the illustration above, part of the flap to the right has responded to dry opening but a spot has been encountered that will not. Put a small amount of water in a Petrie dish. Wet a cotton swab in this dish and then blot it on the piece of blotting paper to remove excess water. Press the swab down on the flap over the difficult spot. Repeat this several times and allow the water to sink in. It may be necessary to use warm water to get results. Use the opening tool to maintain *light* lifting pressure on the flap after it is wet. As the glue softens the flap will lift.

STEAM OPENINGS

Where no evidence exists that steam or high temperatures will damage the envelope or letter, the steam opening is the most expeditious and incidentally is probably the most commonly used method for surreptitious letter openings.

The amount of steam used is quite important. Steam can alter the characteristics of the paper and therefore should be used as sparingly as possible. On the other hand, too little steam might result in tearing of the paper fibers. It is important to study the technique shown in the following carefully and to develop skill through plenty of practice before beginning operational work as the first attempt may appear very easy and subsequent envelopes may be much harder.

Envelopes of thin paper will not require as much steam and indeed cannot tolerate much steam without bleeding. Therefore, the flap must be lifted as soon as the adhesive loosens, but because the paper is weakened by the steam the lifting force must be light. Envelopes of heavy paper will require more steam and can tolerate more lifting force.

There are two basic ways of performing steam openings. One is to apply a lifting force with the opening tool to the end of the flap and apply steam to the flap near the tool until it lefts for a space of about one inch. The opening tool is then moved under the flap to the unopened spot and steam is again applied. These steps are repeated until the envelope is opened. When manipulating envelopes of manila or other heavy paper, the lifting method is usually best as the heavy glue on such envelopes tends to bind on the opening tool preventing it from sliding smoothly. This technique is not desirable for thin paper envelopes as it tends to stretch the flap of such envelopes unevenly making them appear wrinkled.

The second technique is to hold the opening tool in a fixed position relative to the steam jet and to move the envelope across the tool. The steam is applied just ahead of the tool and the envelope is moved in a smooth continuous motion at a speed determined by the rate at which the adhesive loosens. This technique usally produces the best results but requires more practice than the former.

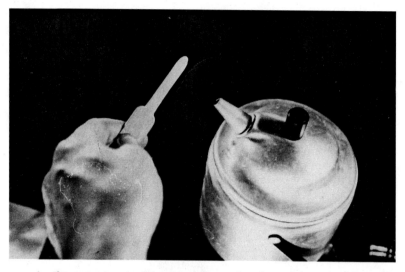

As the opening tool is naturally cooler than the steam jet, the steam will condense on its surface at first and form droplets or a film of water. This water will wet the envelope unnecessarily and can cause bleeding of the glue.

To prevent this condensation from effecting the envelope, bring the temperature of the tool up to that of the steam by holding the tool in the steam jet as shown for about ten seconds. Then wipe the water off with a cloth or the fingers. Use this process each time the tool is used and make it a habit. It has the advantage of minimizing the chances of bleeding and also tends to keep the tool clean.

To perform the steam opening, place the right hand holding the tool as shown and keep it there. Bring the opening at the end of the flap down onto the tip of the tool with the left hand. This

will bring the sealed part of the flap at the extreme right end of the envelope into the jet of steam. As the adhesive loosens, move the left hand to the right. Gradually shift the bottom of the envelope away from the steamer so that the tool is at the angle to the envelope shown in the picture. This separates the opened flap from the envelope and keeps it from resealing itself to the right of the tool. When the left hand gets too close for comfort to the steamer, move both hands away from the steamer and shift the left hand to the left on the envelope and move the tool and envelope back to the vicinity of the steamer. Be very careful during this process not to push the tool up inside the flap beyond the glue line as glue on the tool will leave marks on the inside of the slap as evidence of the opening work. When the envelope is open, hold the flap away from the envelope until the flue has hardened somewhat, otherwise the envelope may re-seal itself.

Cut a piece of blotting paper to the size of the top of the "Grill" being used and wet it by flowing water across its surface. Do *not* soak it.

Lay the blotter on the "Grill" and increase the temperature until the steam can be barely seen rising from the surface of the blotter. The right temperature setting of the thermostat will vary

15

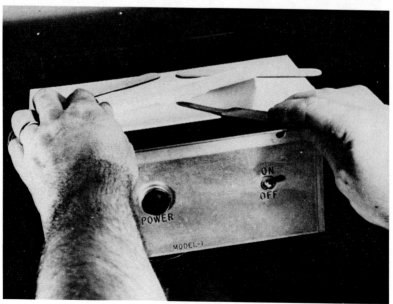

with altitude but should in any case be set through trial-and-error on non-operational material.

The envelope is then placed flap down on the blotter. If the corners at the top lift up they may be held down *lightly* with weights as shown.

After 15-30 seconds, lift up the bottom edge of the envelope with the left hand and see if the point of the flap is loose by pulling it down with *very* gentle pressure with an opening tool. If it is loose, hold the tip of the flap gently against the blotter with the opening tool and lift the envelope up. It should open easily. If its does not, leave it for a few more seconds and try again.

WAX SEALS

The wax seal is a device put across the flap line of an envelope to prevent it from being opened surreptitiously by unauthorized persons. The bar of wax is heated until it becomes a gummy liquid and is applied in that form to suitable spots on the flap line. A metal stamp is then pressed into the molten wax leaving an impression with a distinctive and usually complex pattern.

In making a surreptitious entry into an envelope protected by such seals, the procedure outlined in the following pages is usually successful.

It is almost impossible to duplicate a seal exactly even if the original stamp is available. Therefore, if a sufficiently good photograph of the seal on an envelope were sent to the same addressee through a separate mail channel it would probably be possible to determine if a seal had been manipulated by comparing the seal on the envelope with the photograph. It is most unlikely that such precautions would be taken but the possibility must be kept in mind.

There have been cases where waxes of different colors have been used to make up one seal. These cannot be melted and reused as the colors will blend differently during the process. Such seals can be manipulated if a new set of waxes are used but an assortment of colors of the *same kind* of wax must be available in such cases and the protective photo system would reveal the manipulation as the color patterns in the seal can never be duplicated exactly.

Fortunately, elaborate precautions in mail channels are unusual and the following techniques will usually suffice.

Needless to say, the operator should have as much practice as possible on non-operational material before attempting a manipulation of wax seals on operational mail. This is a difficult process and it usually only attempted by experts on opposition mail. When the operator has had this type of training and has practiced as much as possible it will usually be his own decision to determine if he is ready when the requirement arises. Therefore he should practice as often as he can on various types of seals so that he will not have to pass up an opportunity when it does arise. Remember, the letters with the seals are the ones that contain something good.

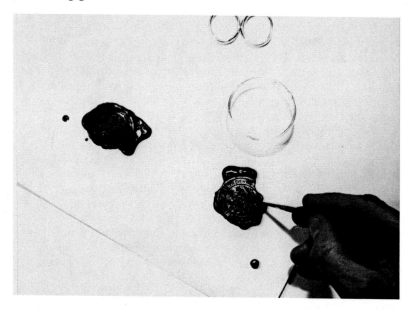

Before embarking on an effort of this kind it should be ascertained that sufficient time is available. One hour is a safe minimum if all equipment and material is set up and ready for use.

The thickest, clearest, and most complete seals are the easiest to copy so the best one from that point of view should be selected for manipulation.

Put some mineral oil in a Petrie dish and brush a *thin* coating of it over the face of the seal. Do *not* get oil on the paper.

Add one level teaspoon of water to three level teaspoons of lightly packed Albastone powder in a rubber mixing cup. Surface tension can cause a teaspoon to hold more than one level tea-spoonful of water so be sure the water is level across the top of the teaspoon. Stir the mixture with a tongue depresser for 4 to 6 minutes. The mixture should be thick enough so that it will not flow off the edge of the seal but thin enough to fill in around the features of the pattern. If necessary a small amount of powder or water may be added to the mixture to bring it to the proper consistency but only a *very small* amount should be added. Any such additions should be made within three minutes of the original mixing to allow plenty of stirring time. Be sure there are no lumps of powder in the mixture before pouring. This powder is not difficult to mix and the amount of stirring indicated will invariably produce a good mixture providing dry powder is not left around the edges of the cup.

Using the tongue depresser, apply a little of the mixture at a time to the face of the seal. Use a second tongue depresser to push with if necessary. Do not let the mixture flow off the edge of the

19

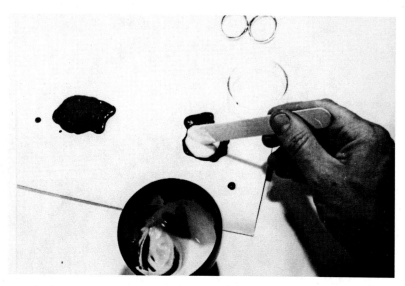

seal onto the paper. Cover just a part of the seal containing the impression if possible. Keep adding plaster and build up the mold until it is about an inch thick with sides as vertical as possible. If the weight of the plaster that is added to attain this thickness tends to push the bottom layer out off the edge of the pattern, wait until eleven minutes after the initial mixture of powder and water before building up the thickness of the mold. As an example, pour the mixture into the seal and get the pattern covered with a layer approximately one-eighth inch thick. Then wait until eleven minutes have passed since the mixture of powder and water was combined and then add a new mixture of thicker plaster to back up the bottom layer. The mold is made thick primarily for strength, so build it up straight up from the edges.

The timing given above is predicated on the fact that the Albastone will begin to harden ten minutes after it is mixed with water no matter what the proportion and gets hard in a matter of seconds.

Before removing the mold from the seal, make a pencil mark on the mold on the three points opposite the flap lines. This is done so that the seal can be oriented properly when it is replaced. Wait twenty minutes from the time the water was first mixed with the powder and then lift the mold from the seal.

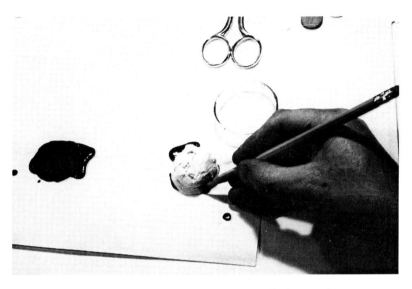

Brush or otherwise clean off any particles of plaster that may have stuck to the seal.

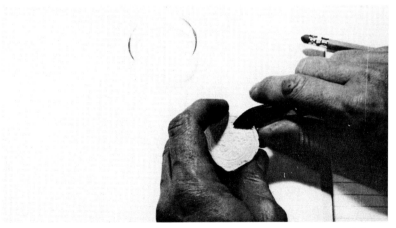

Scrape off any parts of the impression that are not part of the seal pattern. The final mold should look like the face of the original stamp if a complete seal is copied. Place the mold face down in the oil in the Petrie dish and let it soak there.

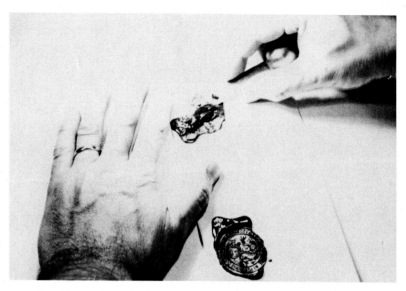

Heat the seal with the infra red lamp, being careful not to scorch the envelope or melt the other seal. Aluminum foil may be wrapped around the part of the envelope not being manipulated as protection against the heat.

When the wax softens, push it up from the edges to the center and form it into a ball. Pick the ball of wax up and set it aside.

Clean off as much of the wax as possible from the paper around and over the glue line on the flap and then open that end of the envelope using whatever method is appropriate.

After examination of the contents of the envelope and re-sealing it in the appropriate manner put it on the table in front of the infra red lamp. Take the mold out of the oil and clean off excess oil with a soft cloth. Apply heat to the ball of wax on the place where the seal was originally and as the wax softens guide it into the proper outline of the original pattern. Keep the wax very thin in the areas where the pattern was incomplete. Then soften the wax well.

Push the mold down into the wax being very careful to line up the guide marks properly. Apply enough pressure only to make a good impression but do not force the wax out from under the edge of the mold where it had not been previously.

Wait about two minutes for the wax to cool and then remove the mold. Clean any particles of plaster that might have fallen off the mold from the seal. It may be advisable to brush a light film of oil over the face of the copy if it is not as shiny as the other but this should be done with discretion as both seals can change appearance during handling in normal channels.

REPAIRS

Damage caused during the surreptitious entry can take many forms. The two basic types that can be successfully repaired are torn paper fibers and bleeding of the glue through the paper. Other repairs may be possible but these will depend upon the time available and the ingenuity of the operator. Fibers of paper may be pulled up from the surface of the envelope or flap so that they stand up or they may be torn loose so that they adhere to the opposite surface and leave thin spots in the paper from which they were torn. Bleeding is a term used to describe the glue soaking through the paper to the opposite surface. This happens more easily on thin spots in the paper than in areas of normal thickness. Therefore torn fibers can show up on the outside of the envelope as places where glue has bled through the flap. It should be remembered however that bleeding can occur in both the flap and the envelope and careful inspection by the rightful recipient of the envelope could reveal either. The most common (and avoidable) cause of bleeding is excessive wetting of the paper either during opening or resealing.

Certain types of damage and repair techniques are shown in the following pages.

This tear in the bottom flap occurred when this part of the flap was out of sight beneath the top flap. It was caused by the opening tool, which got caught under the bottom flap during the opening. There is very little that can be done to repair this except to glue it back down in its original place. Glue should be used in such cases with great discretion.

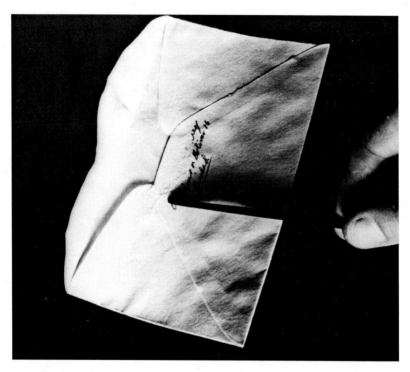

This is an example of a very bad case of torn fibers. The more usual case would be one of two or three fibers standing up from the surface from which they were pulled. Fibers are usually pulled up because insufficient steam was used during the opening. Torn or pulled up fibers can betray a surreptitious entry if the recipient is observant. On the other hand, envelopes can partially seal themselves in storage prior to use and then be torn slightly when opened for use. Self-sealing usually is more prevalent in hot, damp climates. For this reasons some envelopes are sold with very little glue on them and the sender will always add glue or cellophane tape to seal them more effectively.

Pulled up fibers may usually be tamped down into place providing the damage is moderate. Use a damp swab and tamp lightly, pushing the fibers in the appropriate direction.

Fibers that are torn off and are only held on the paper by the glue should be rubbed off with a damp swab.

Remember that paper that has been roughened by this kind of damage is more likely to bleed than normal paper. Therefore, use a minimum of water or glue on such spots.

This is an example of bleeding. In envelopes of thin paper some bleeding may be apparent along the glue line and usually may be ignored. Spot bleeding is usually caused by manipulation and can betray the entry to the recipient of the letter.

Light bleeding may sometimes be removed by wetting the spot and then pressing a dry blotter to it. This process is repeated several times in rapid succession.

In more severe cases it is advisable to remove all glue from the flap. This is done by sandwiching the flap as shown above between two damp (not wet) blotters and pressing a hot iron down on them so that the glue is steamed out. Turn the envelope over and repeat this until all glue is off the flap. Then iron the paper dry and apply glue in a very thin coat and with care to follow the original glue line.

Be careful not to steam out any writing or seals on the flap line or to change the color of any pattern that may exist in the paper.

If a thick paper liner exists inside the envelope and the flap, it should be removed carefully before this repair work is done. When replacing the liner be sure to add glue only to spots where it originally existed.

Re-SEALING

Re-sealing the envelope properly is as important as properly opening it. It is desirable to re-seal an envelope with the existing glue if possible. If there is insufficient glue for this it is necessary to add glue carefully in a thin coat following the existing glue line as closely as possible.

The glue that is added should not be noticeably different in color (either under visible or UV light) from that of the existing glue. A fairly fluid and neutral colored glue called 101-X (not commercially available) is recommended for general use.

After re-sealing, the envelope may be ironed flat with a warm iron to take out wrinkles. Never rub the iron on an envelope. *Always* apply the iron through a clean paper or blotter. Ironing sometimes causes the envelope to develop a distinct curl. Pressing the envelope for several hours under a few heavy books is a better approach if time is available.

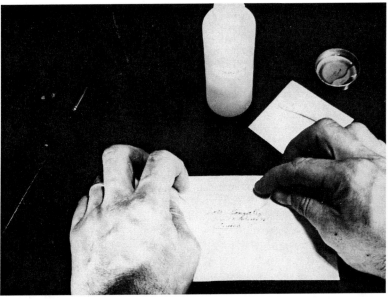

Before wetting the flap or adding glue, hold the envelope flap down in its sealed position to be sure that it will go back into place properly. Stretching of the flap can cause some difficulty in lining up all of the writing or lines of a seal across the flap line.

If any of the writing or stamp on the envelope extends *under* the edge of the flap after it is glued down, it is a dead giveaway of the entry. If the flap is warped or stretched and writing won't line up well, it is better to leave a little space between the flap line and the lines on the body of the envelope than to allow the lines to get under the edge of the flap.

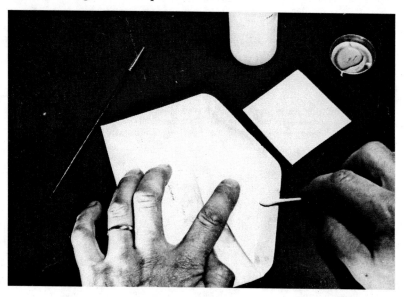

Put water into a Petrie dish. Wet a cotton swab and then remove excess water from it on a blotter so that the swab is wet but not soaked.

ROLL the swab along the glue line and on any spots on the body of the envelope where glue appears. Immediately fold the flap down into place, observing the aforementioned precautions.

As mentioned previously, glue may be necessary. If so, use it in a Petrie dish and avoid using an excessive amount. It is sometimes desirable to mix glue and water so that a thin coating may be applied to envelopes of thin paper. Make the mixture in very small quantities in a Petrie dish.

Don't wet the flap with your tongue. A little poison in the original glue would be a fine way to thin the ranks of the opposition. This approach has not been heard of yet as an opposition technique but who wants to be the first to discover it the hard way?

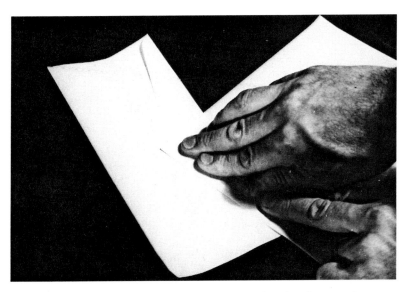

After the flap is in place, press it down firmly after putting a piece of clean paper over the flap. Use firm steady pressure. Do not rub more than once or twice across the flap. Sustained pressure without rubbing does the most good when a minimum of adhesive is used.

If there are unstuck spots after this step, they may be moistened slightly with the No. 1 brush and water. Use the water sparingly and hold the spot down under a piece of paper for approximately 30 seconds.

TRAPS

Traps are used by the sender to enable the recipient to determine if his letter has been opened during its time in transit. There must usually be a prearranged agreement between the correspondents to enable them to recognize each others traps.

31

Traps may be overt or covert. The overt trap, when sprung, will be evident to the surreptitious opener while the covert type will not if it is successful.

The good trap is one that cannot be discovered before the envelope is opened. It must also leave conclusive evidence when it has been sprung, otherwise it is worse than useless.

COMMON TYPES OF OVERT TRAPS

Carbon paper wrapped around the letter inside the envelope
Wax paper used the same way
Marks with an indelible pencil under or near the glue line
Gluing part of the letter to the envelope
Spots of powdered dye in the flue under the flap

Covert traps usually involve the use of some type of SW (secret writing) across the flap. They may also take the form of a bit of repairable damage to the envelope that the clandestine operator might repair thinking that he had caused it. It could also take the form of an unglued section of the flap that the conscientious operator might reseal.

It should be remembered that a letter is subjected to many kinds of treatment and environmental conditions in normal mail channels that could possibly spring a trap. Therefore, a good deal of common sense must be used in manipulating trapped envelopes.

THE PROCEDURE FOR SURREPTITIOUS OPENINGS

In the course of the operator's career he will encounter many letters for manipulation. He should never consider any of these as routine and take short cuts or get careless. The most innocuous looking envelope may be the one that will get the operator in the most trouble.

The procedure outlined in the following will reveal most traps and although it takes a few minutes it is well worth the trouble.

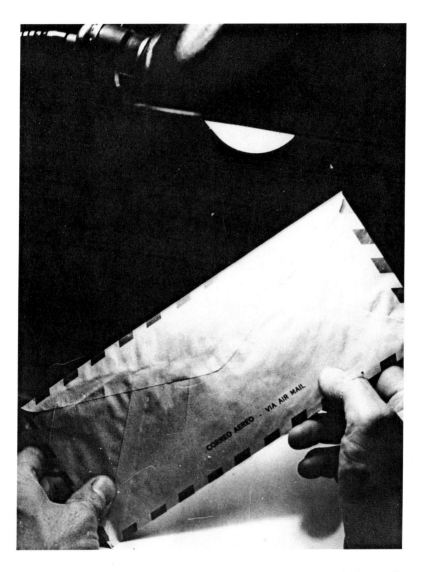

Examine the exterior of the envelope under a strong light at all angles. Look for unusual features that might be traps.

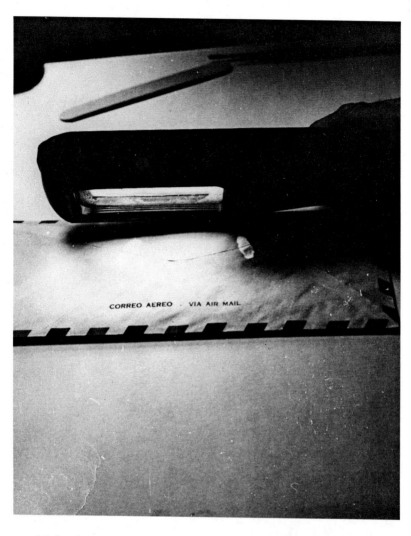

Make the same examination of all parts of the envelope under UV light for any indications of a trap. In the photo above the marks visible under UV light were not visible at all in ordinary light.

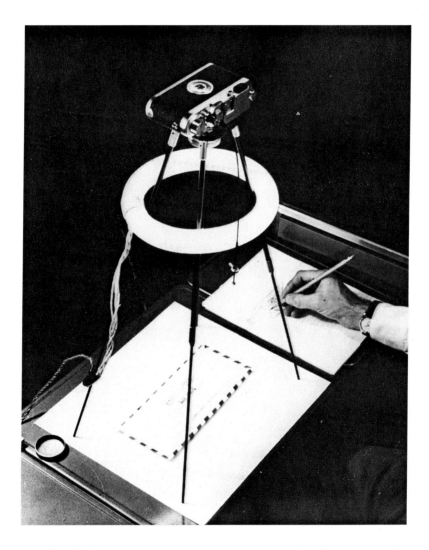

Sketch the envelope showing any pertinent details that should be remembered during re-sealing. Photograph the envelope front and back so that the photos of the contents can be correlated with the addressee and addressor as shown on the envelope.

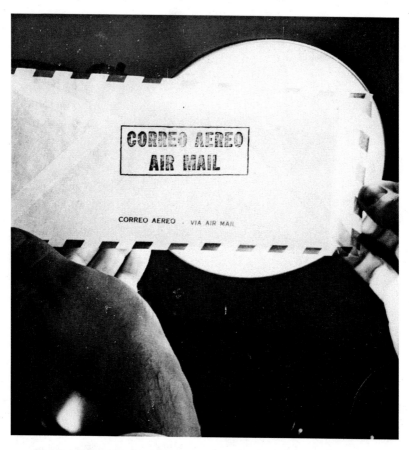

Look at the envelope in front of a strong light so that its contents are outlined.

Shake the envelope to see if the letter is glued in place
Look for traps under the seams, etc.
Look for specks of dye, etc. that might spread when steamed
Look for wax or carbon paper inside the envelope

Make every attempt to determine the nature of the contents of the envelope to see if they will be affected by the opening procedures such as wetting or steaming, etc.

A trap was revealed by this check. See it?

Lightly make two small pencil marks across each side of the flap to be opened. These will be used to line up the seal during the re-sealing process. They are important in the event that SW lines are drawn across the seams as a trap.

The safest opening method in the presence of traps is probably the dry opening but it should be done with extreme caution as one trap type is extra glue such as rice paste or water glass on spots in the other glue on the flap. These spots can easily cause tearing during either a steam or dry opening.

Wetting with water over the glue is successful in many cases where heat from steam of the grill can spring a trap. Care should be taken to avoid feathering the ink inside the letter by wetting it. Wax, carbon, or thermofax paper will be seriously effected by heat.

When the flap has been opened the letter should be examined carefully before attempts are made to remove it to see if it is glued in place.

As the letter is removed from the envelope, make one or more sketches showing the manner in which it is folded and its orientation in the envelope.

Photograph the contents being careful not to mix the pages up.

Replace the contents exactly as they were originally and re-seal the envelope using the appropriate technique.

The operator may wear gloves while handling the contents of the envelope if he suspects that the presence of his fingerprints may be the trap.

EXAMINATION OF RECEIVED MAIL

The purpose of this type of examination is to determine as accurately as possible whether or not an envelope has been covertly opened during its transit time between addresser and addressee. It is assumed in the following that there have been no prearranged traps made in the subject material.

The following steps are given in the order in which they should be carried out. Under this procedure, several things may become evident during the examination that will not prove conclusively that the envelope has been opened covertly. All evidence should be noted however, and the overall results of the examination considered when making a decision.

1. An external visual examination should be carried out prior to opening the envelope. Any of the following should be noted:
a. Wrinkles and whether they are pressed in or not. These might have occurred through normal handling or during a covert opening by an inept operator.
b. Tears in the flap.
c. Bleeding of the glue. This may be normal with envelopes on thin paper. Bleeding in isolated spots in the flap should be suspected especially where the envelope is of heavy paper.
d. Smudging or tearing in the area of the flap indicating considerable handling. This could happen during normal handling or during a covert opening by an inept operator.
e. Misaligned cachets or writing across the flap. If definitely misaligned this can be fairly conclusive evidence especially if part of the cachet is under the flap.
f. Flattened ridges due to ironing. This may also happen due to the type of handling in the mail.
g. A thin line of glue extending out from under the flap. This is the original glue line and shows that the flap was not re-glued in its original position.
h. Any of the above phenomena occurring with regard to the bottom or ends of the envelope.
i. Feathering of the ink due to steaming of the flap.
j. Excessive flatness and curling (usually concave when looking at the back.

2. An external visual examination should be performed under UV light. The following things should be noted if they appear:
a. Excessive glue appearing from under the flaps. This could happen on the top flap if the sender added glue and was slightly sloppy but would rarely happen on the end flap seams of a normal business size envelope.
b. Two kinds of glue appearing under the flaps. Same possibility as above.
c. A difference in fluorescence between the paper, design on

the paper or the ink in the front and the other parts of the envelope that might have been steamed or otherwise manipulated during an opening.

3. The envelope should be tested for SW or marks across the flap or flaps using the appropriate technique.

4. The envelope should be steamed at one point near the flap for approximately 15 seconds. It should then be examined under UV light to see if there is a difference in fluorescence between that spot and the unsteamed part of the envelope. If there is a difference and such a difference does not appear on other parts of the flap it would tend to indicate that the flap had not been previously steamed.

5. The envelope should now be opened by slitting it along one *surface* near the edge. None of the flaps nor an edge should be cut to get the contents out.

6. After the contents of the envelope have been removed, examine the inside of the envelope for:
   a. Tears in the flap.
   b. Glue smudges that might have been caused during a covert opening.
   c. Bleeding.

7. Repeat step (6) above with a UV light source.

8. The envelope should now be completely opened by thorough steaming of all the flaps. Care should be taken to prevent tearing and smudging of the glue during this process. The edges should be tested for a French opening during the steaming. (A French opening is one where the end of the envelope is sliced off with scissors. It is re-sealed with a narrow layer of glue that just holds the ends of the opening together. It is not a recommended technique because when discovered there is no doubt that the mail was covertly opened. The French call this a British opening.)

9. After opening, examine the flaps very carefully for torn fibers,

torn paper and an extra layer of glue applied with care over the original layer. (A person adding glue normally will not use such care.) Repeat this examination under UV light.

The decision as to whether or not a given envelope has been covertly opened may be very important at some time in the future. An expert at surreptitious entries will leave little or no trace of his work, and therefore such a decision will usually be very difficult and must be stated objectively unless there is conclusive evidence one way or the other.

I.D.1.1

MANIPULATION OF CELLOPHANE TAPE
(F & S Procedure)

The purpose of this paper is to describe a procedure for the manipulation of cellophane tape during clandestine mail intercepts.

This technique was devised because an operational requirement arose for the manipulation of this type of tape that began to appear on target mail that was accessible for a relatively short time. This mail had characteristics that required precise placement of the tape when it was re-applied. The technique is quick, safe, and permits a high degree of accuracy in replacement of the tape. Therefore, it is recommended for all operational work of this kind.

This paper was prepared for use by properly trained technical operations specialists. It is to accompany Section I.D.I of the MK-CHARITY Operations Manual.

GENERAL CONSIDERATIONS

Frequently, only a portion of the cellophane tape protecting the envelope is removed during a clandestine opening. This is done to facilitate its replacement in the proper position and to save time in general.

There are cases however, where there are other complicated manipulations to be performed on the same envelope that might be interfered with if strips of tape were only partially removed. In such cases, removal of all of the tape is highly desirable.

The system described, while not revolutionary in any respect, is quite effective. It has been found possible to replace cellophane tape in which inked fingerprints and raised letters were impressed, with excellent results. Moreover, the technique does not require very extensive practice for good proficiency.

Handling the tape with glass rods and procelain spatulas does not seem to effect it adversely. Placing the tape on a sheet of glass also is not detrimental and certainly has advantages.

Contrary to normally advocated procedure, all work involving cellophane tape should be performed on a glass covered table top. The table top should be covered with a blotter however, after the cellophane tape has been put in storage on the glass sheet and then removed when the tape is to be replaced.

As in other phases of F & S work cleanliness is of the utmost importance. The adhesive on cellophane tape collects dust and dirt like a magnet. Therefore, the tools and glass sheet must be completely clean. The glass sheet used for storage of the cellophane tape should be cleaned with a detergent and water and then dried with a clean cloth just before the work. When the tape has been removed, a certain amount of the adhesive will remain on the envelope. This will become dirty with handling. That part of the envelope should be protected with a sheet of clean aluminum foil or should be cleaned with a soft rubber eraser before the tape is replaced. The former or a combination of the two procedures is desirable.

Although the procedure to be described makes this type of manipulation easier, there should be no relaxation of alertness during the work. The tape can split, and if not observed immediately, can be a serious problem. Other things can also happen that require immediate attention and counter action. For that reason the greatest of care must be taken throughout this process.

MATERIAL REQUIRED

1 Plate Glass Sheet 16 x 20 x 1 /4"	1 Hypodermic Needle No. 20
1 Plate Glass Sheet 8 x 10 x 1/4"	1 Surgical Hemostat
1 Porcelain Spatula 4 x 1/2"	1 Hypodermic Syringe 3cc
12 Glass Rod 3 x 3/16"	1 Petrie Dish 1 1/2 x 3/8"
1 Camel Hair Brush No. 2	1 No. 4H Pencil
1 Bottle Carbon Tetrachloride 2 oz	1 6" Plastic Ruler

Sketch the layout of the tape on the envelope. Number the strips of tape on the sketch in the order in which they will be replaced. Put the sketch under the sheet of glass that will be used for storage of the tape.

Mark the end and one point along the edge of the tape using a No. 4H pencil. Mark lightly but carefully so that there will be no doubt later on the exact location of the tape.

Put the drop of carbon tetrachloride on the paper at the end of the tape that will be removed first. Be sure that it is the uppermost layer of tape.

When using a hypodermic needle for this step, use a very small amount of carbon tetrachloride and support the plunger with the thumb and index finger. Otherwise, the weight of the plunger by itself will force the liquid from the syringe.

Attach the edge of the jaw of a hemostat to the end of the tape. Grip only the minimum amount of tape necessary. Use the clamp of the hemostat to maintain the pressure on the tape.

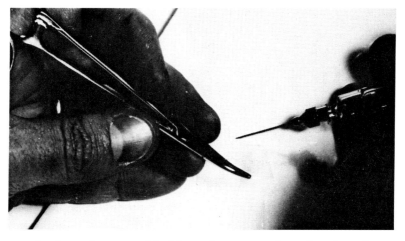

Apply carbon tetrachloride to the paper using a brush or the hypodermic needle in the normal manner and lift the tape for a distance of two inches. Let the tape dry for at least 30 seconds and then attach a spatula to it as shown in the following illustration.

The tape should be applied firmly to the spatula and then held in place with the thumb. Although the end of the spatula is smooth and round the tape should not be pulled down and across the end. The tape should always be pulled directly off the end of the spatula.

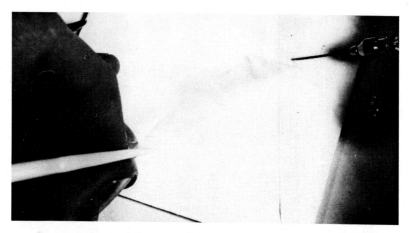

Remove most of the rest of the tape in the usual manner. Do not put carbon tetrachloride on the tape where it overlaps another strip of tape as it will leave too much adhesive residue. Pull the tape off the layer below but watch very carefully that the tape does not split or break.

Notice the appearance and location of the pencil marks on this illustration.

Just before the end of the strip of tape comes loose from the envelope wait at least 30 seconds and then attach a piece of glass tubing to the tape about ½″ from its end.

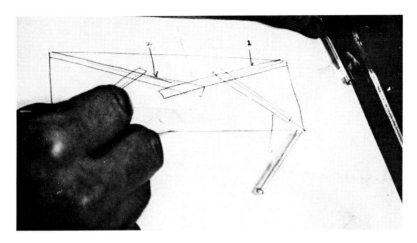

Lay the piece of tape out on the plate glass sheet in the same relative position it occupied on the envelope. Pull the spatula away and put a piece of glass tubing under the end of the tape. Rub the rest of the tape out on the glass to remove any irregularities that might leave marks in the adhesive when the tape is removed from the glass.

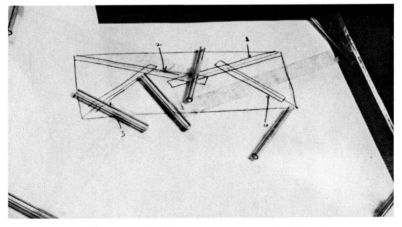

Remove all the tape in the same way and lay it out on the glass in the relative position it occupies on the envelope but do not overlap it.

When the process has reached the point where the tape is to be replaced, attach a piece of celluloid to the end of the first strip of tape to be replaced. Overlap the tape about ½″ on the celluloid.

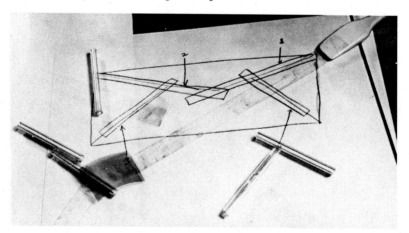

Attach a spatula to the other end of the same strip. The celluloid and spatula are used to handle the tape. With these devices it is possible to handle the tape firmly and to manipulate it with a high degree of accuracy.

Using either the celluloid or the spatula, but not both, pull the tape up from the glass in one continuous motion. If this is not done properly, marks will be left in the tape. Watch very carefully to see that the tape does not split or break during this process.

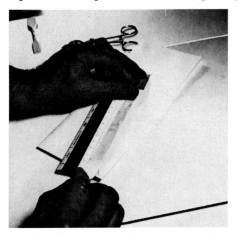

Hold the spatula at least one inch off the envelope while placing the celluloid with the tape on it on the envelope and positioning the tape exactly over the alignment mark made before the tape was removed. Maintain some tension on the tape to keep it taut so that it won't touch the envelope prematurely. When the tape under the celluloid is aligned exactly with the mark on the envelope, move the spatula so that the tape lines up with the second mark. Recheck the position of the tape under the celluloid and then press the tape down against the envelope with the finger of the left hand. Slide the thumb along the tape toward the spatula all the while marking sure that the spatula is holding the tape directly over the alignment mark at the edge of the tape. Keep the envelope flap with the left hand or by using a ruler as shown. Do not put too much tension on the tape as it is being applied as it will stretch and then cause the envelope to curl noticeably after it has been put in place on the envelope.

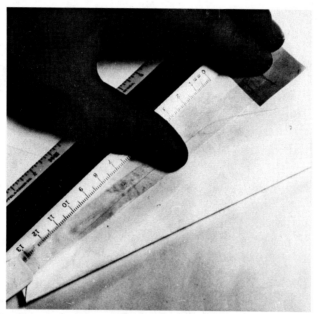

The illustration above shows the alignment mark under the piece of celluloid. It is very important that this step be carried out properly if precision placement of the tape is a requirement. When the tape has been pushed down on the envelope for about an inch, this mark can be ignored and all attention given to the second mark at the spatula end of the tape.

When the entire strip of tape has been attached to the envelope, peel the celluloid off the end of the tape. This is another point where great care should be observed to see that the tape does not split or break.

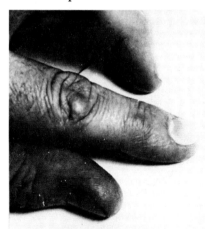

When the celluloid has been removed, *slide* the left index finger along the tape toward its end to attach the tape to the envelope. The mark should line up exactly with the corner of the tape.

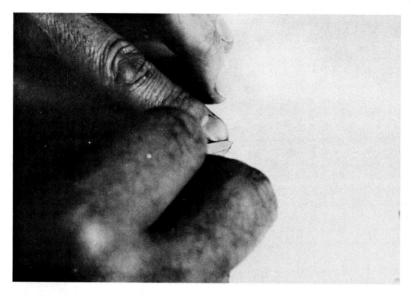

Use the scalpel to clean any dirt that might exist along the edge of the tape. This is especially important along the edge of the bottom layer of tape where another strip of tape overlaps it. Use the scalpel with care to avoid cutting the paper.

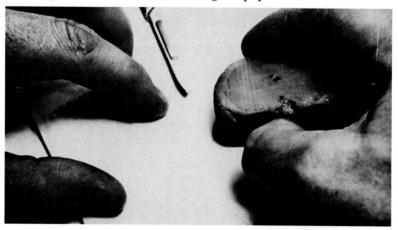

Use a soft eraser to clean all marks and smudges from the envelope.